Katie Clemons
LET'S CELEBRATE YOUR STORY

BETWEEN DAD AND ME

A FATHER & SON
KEEPSAKE JOURNAL

sourcebooks
eXplore

TO TODD AND MICHELLE,
MY FIRST TREE-CLIMBING BUDDIES.
WE REALLY COULD SEE
THE WHOLE WORLD TOGETHER.

NIKLAS'S ART, AGE 4

Published by Sourcebooks eXplore, an imprint of Sourcebooks Kids.
P.O. Box 4410, Naperville, Illinois 60567–4410
(630) 961-3900
sourcebookskids.com

Source of Production: Versa Press, East Peoria, Illinois, USA
Date of Production: February 2021
Run Number: 5021279

Printed and bound in the United States of America.
VP 10 9 8 7 6 5 4 3

A BOY NEEDS HiS DAD

MY FOUR-YEAR-OLD SON, NIKLAS, looked so collected, confident, and strong as he climbed an enormous apple tree...until his foot slipped off the branch. His body flew downward, and his knees banged against branches and scraped against bark. A moment later, he was clinging to a branch as his feet dangled below.

"Get me down, Daddy!" he pleaded. I could hear desperation in his voice and feel my own heart hammering. I instinctively wanted to jump into the scene, but his father—who stood under the tree—said, "It's okay, it's okay!" as he patted a tree limb. "You've still got this. Just put your foot here."

Niklas tentatively swung his right leg to the branch where his father's hand rested. Then his dad tapped another branch, and Niklas placed his other foot there. He didn't wait for the next instruction—or maybe his dad wasn't planning on offering more—instead my son pulled himself up and confidently kept climbing.

Sometimes a boy just needs his dad.

You are your son's hero. As he watches you deal with life's challenges—and sees how you deal with events and how you interact with others—he models his behavior after yours. His character, morals, and sense of self-esteem are all things he learns from you.

When you deal with accidents and losses calmly, and treat others with dignity, you offer an example he can aspire to. And when it's time for him to leap from childhood to adulthood, he'll seek your counsel because you're his dad, the man he admires most.

From a young age, your son craves opportunities to connect with you. Sharing can be hard, but this journal offers an inventive, lively way for you and your son to draw closer as you share stories, adventures, interests, and unique perspectives. As you answer prompts that make you laugh, reflect on each other's lives, or invite conversations on deeper issues, you and your son will climb to a more fulfilling relationship. Journaling is like venturing into a tree together and then watching the world below. It's understanding which tree your son is curious to climb, discussing it together, and then cheering as he works his way up in his own unique style.

I'll never forget the afternoon when Niklas and I returned to that apple tree. He ran right to it and began hoisting himself up, while I started bestowing safety tips: "Hang on tight! Make sure the branch can support you..."

He stopped climbing, turned to me, and said, "Mom, I already know all those things. Dad taught me."

Let this journal be your guide as you climb toward a closer relationship with your son. These five guideposts will help you get the most from your storycatching time together.

❶ WRITE YOUR OWN RULES.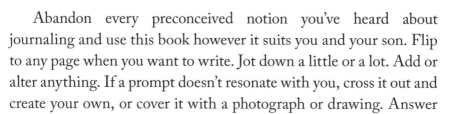

Abandon every preconceived notion you've heard about journaling and use this book however it suits you and your son. Flip to any page when you want to write. Jot down a little or a lot. Add or alter anything. If a prompt doesn't resonate with you, cross it out and create your own, or cover it with a photograph or drawing. Answer the questions together under a shady tree, or pass the book back and forth, making entries in turn.

Your son's thoughts go on pages that begin "Dear Son" or "Son Writes." Corresponding "Dear Dad" and "Dad Writes" pages are your opportunity to reply or launch another conversation. Intermixed throughout are spaces to write, doodle, and adhere mementos.

❷ LISTEN FULLY.

Sharing this journal grants you and your son a peek inside one another's heads and hearts. While you may feel tempted to lecture or point out his faults in these pages, try to understand what your son is really communicating. Does he want you to change things for him, or does he actually just need you to lend an ear as he sorts stuff out?

Some pages might spur stories from your own childhood. Others can help you discover emotions, perspectives, or entire events that you weren't aware of—from him or yourself. Your son may have things he would like to say but isn't comfortable communicating yet. Give him time and keep listening. And when he chooses to share something difficult, don't feel like you must respond immediately. Give yourself time to think and find the best way to acknowledge what your son trusted you enough to relate.

❸ SHARE YOUR HONEST iDEAS.

A great story doesn't have to be perfect to be impactful, and neither do you. Your son wants to know what you think and feel, especially about him. Tell your stories, model your values, and demonstrate that imperfection in both life and writing is okay.

My journals are sprinkled with inventive spelling, scribbled out words, and sentences that slowly fade across the page as the pen I'm using runs out of ink. But I keep writing because I have found that jotting down some story—no matter how insignificant my thoughts may seem—is infinitely better than sharing nothing.

❹ GET MESSY.

Write and play on these pages. Express yourselves with stick figures, arrows, and doodles. Adhere photographs and keepsakes. Tuck in ticket stubs from some event you experienced together. Emphasize ideas by underlining words, writing in all caps, or experimenting with different pens. Trace your hands. Add captions and fake mustaches to the illustrations. Splatter paint on a page. Rotate your journal 180 degrees and write upside down, or keep pivoting it as you write in a spiral. Above all, enjoy yourselves.

❺ GO BEYOND THESE PAGES.

Your father-son journaling experience only begins with this journal. Come explore my exclusive *Between Dad and Me* resources, which include unexpected ways to swap top-secret messages in this book, journaling jokes your son will love, and examples from my own journals on:

KATIECLEMONS.COM/A/AGTN

I'd love to hear how your journal is coming together. Please drop me a note at **howdy@katieclemons.com** (I answer all my mail) or join me on social media **@katierclemons**, **#katieclemonsjournals**, and **#betweendadandme**.

Imagine picking up this journal in ten or twenty years or handing it to your grown son. You'll be taken back in time as you see pages filled with stories and perspectives that have long-since changed, youthful penmanship recording moments you haven't thought about in years, photographs, illustrations, and best of all…reminders of how much you love each other.

YOU'RE A GREAT DAD. Grab a blanket, spread it beneath the stars, and… Let's celebrate your story! ♡ Katie

Here's a photograph or drawing of
YOU  & ME

HELLO **UNIVERSE!**

Our full names are

_____

_____

We sign our names like this

_____

_____

We call each other

_____

_____

We are _____ and _____ years old.

TODAY, WE LAUNCH THIS JOURNAL!

 Date_____

OUR JOURNAL
GUIDELINES

1 Is our journal top secret or can anyone else look inside?

2 If someone finds this journal, they should

☐ Return it

☐ Complete it

☐ Destroy it

☐ Share pages online

☐ Hide it in _____

☐ Sell it for $ _____

☐ Turn it into a _____ movie

3 Do we have to answer prompts in numerical order?

☐ Yes   ☐ No

4 Our top focus(es) in this journal will be to

☐ Express our thoughts

☐ Use perfect grammar

☐ Capture memories

☐ Skip our responsibilities such as _____

_____ in order to write

☐ _____

☐ _____

5 How much time do we have to write before passing our journal back to one another?

6 What could we do if we need more space to write?

7 Is there a specific date when this journal must be complete?

8 How do we pass our journal back and forth?

9 How should we tell each other which page to turn to?

10 How can we communicate when we need an urgent response?

11 Are there other guidelines we should establish for our journal?

DEAR **DAD,**

What's something I do that makes you smile?

DEAR SON,

What's something I do that makes you smile?

TIME FOR
A HIGH FIVE!!

YOU  ME

What we look like eating

DAD

SON

What we look like sleeping

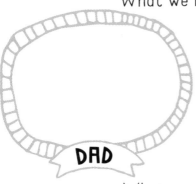

DAD

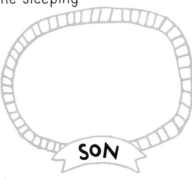

SON

What we look like running

DAD

SON

WE WRITE

DEAR **SON,**

What are three of your most amazing accomplishments?

1

2

3

Is there another goal you want to achieve?

DEAR **DAD,**

What are your thoughts on what I wrote about my achievements?

What do you think of the goal I hope to accomplish?

SON WRITES

Dad, the first thing you say to me in the morning is

The last thing you say to me before bed is

DAD WRITES

Son, the first thing you say to me in the morning is

The last thing you say to me before bed is

SON WRITES

Our family

Our community

Outside our house

Inside our house

DAD WRITES

Our family

Our community

Outside our house

Inside our house

COOL THINGS WE'VE DONE

1

2

3

4

WE WRITE

EXCITING THINGS WE STILL NEED TO DO

TOGETHER

1

2

3

4

DEAR ★ SON,

What do you think it means to be a man?

Do you ever see men acting in a different way?
What do you think about that?

SON WRITES

Here's a picture of you,

MY _____ DAD.

This is you

- ☐ belly laughing
- ☐ being brave
- ☐ acting silly
- ☐ handing me _____
- ☐ attempting great things

- ☐ loving me, your son
- ☐ looking serious
- ☐ spreading joy
- ☐ _____
- ☐ _____

DEAR DAD,

What do you think it means to be a man?
And what do you think about what I wrote?

Do you ever see men acting in a different way?
What do you think about that?

Here's a picture of you,

MY _____ SON.

This is you

- [ ] belly laughing
- [ ] being brave
- [ ] acting silly
- [ ] doing chores without reminders
- [ ] attempting great things
- [ ] looking serious
- [ ] spreading joy
- [ ] loving me, your dad
- [ ] _____

SON ✦ WRITES

I look forward to the holiday season because

_____

_____

_____

I remember one time when

_____

_____

_____

_____

_____

_____

One of my favorite traditions is

_____

_____

_____

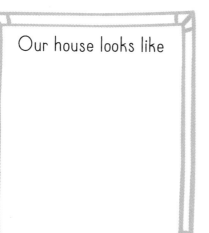

Our house looks like

Our house smells like

People who make the season magical

I love these food traditions

☆ DAD WRITES ☆

When I was growing up, I remember looking
forward to the holiday season because

_____

_____

_____

I remember one time when

_____

_____

_____

_____

_____

_____

One of my favorite traditions was

_____

_____

_____

Our house looked like

Our house smelled like

People who made the season magical

I still cherish the memory of these foods

DEAR **SON,**

Tell me about a time when you knew you did the right thing.

AWESOME SPOT TO DRAW.

HIGH FIVE!

Why did you do it?

How did it make you feel?

COOL!

DEAR **DAD,**

What are your thoughts on choosing to do the right thing?

GREAT SPOT
TO DOODLE.

Do you have a story of when you saw
me doing the right thing?

SUPER

YOU & ME

Right now we're wearing

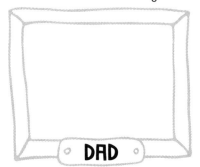

DAD

SON

We're working on

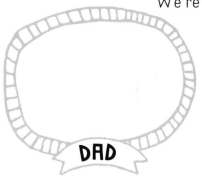

DAD

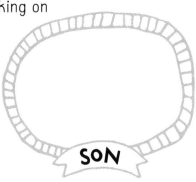

SON

We're probably forgetting

DAD

SON

☆ DAD WRITES ☆

Son, I admire these traits in you

1 _____

_____

2 _____

_____

3 _____

_____

SON ☆ WRITES

Dad, I admire these traits in you

1 _____

_____

2 _____

_____

3 _____

_____

DEAR **DAD,**

What were you like when you were my age?
What was your life like?

DEAR **SON,**

How are you and your life different from
and similar to when I was a kid?

DEAR DAD,

Tell me a story or two about when I was little.

Date

TIME TO SAY
"I LOVE YOU!"

DEAR **SON,**

How do you believe girls and women deserve
to be treated by men?

Do you ever see men doing something different?
How do you feel about that?

DEAR **DAD,**

What are your thoughts on what I wrote?

How do you believe girls and women
deserve to be treated?

Here's a picture of

YOU  &  ME

relishing winter.

We give winter ☆ ☆ ☆ ☆ ☆ stars!

FILL IN FOR
RATING.

WE WRITE

☐ We love this season!

☐ Okay, winter gets kinda long.

Brrrr!

☐ LET IT SNOW!

☐ We should move somewhere _____er.

☐ We have/haven't had enough snow days.

☐ Pour us another mug of _____.

☐ We can't feel our toes.

☐ Winter is warm here!

☐ _____

Our winter theme song should be

♫♪

The best things to do each winter are

1 _____

2 _____

3 _____

4 _____

5 _____

DEAR **DAD,**

Tell me about a time when you realized
you'd made a mistake.

How did it make you feel?

What did you do about it?

Do you think there's anything I should know about making mistakes?

DEAR
SON,

What do you think about what I wrote?

Tell me about a time when you realized
you made a mistake.

How did it make you feel?

What did you do about it?

Is there anything I can do to help you
the next time that happens?

TIME FOR
A HUG!

Date

DEAR **DAD,**

Tell me about a special gift I made you
when I was younger. Do you still have it?

Could you draw a picture?

DEAR
SON,

What kinds of things do you like to make now?

Could you draw a picture?

YOU ♥ ME

Our favorite weekend breakfast

Our most dreaded dinner

Our give-me-seconds most preferred dessert

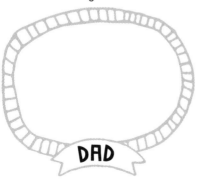

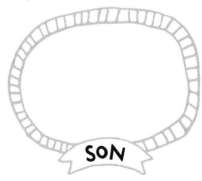

YOU & ME

If we could have any superpower

DAD

SON

DEAR **SON,**

Do you ever feel different from everyone else?

Do you believe that being unlike others
is good or bad in your situation?

Is there anything you'd like from me?

DEAR **DAD,**

What are your thoughts on what
I wrote about feeling different?

Do you ever feel like you're unlike everyone else?

Do you think being different is good or bad?
And how did you form that conclusion?

SON WRITES

Dad, I know you love me so much because

DAD WRITES

Son, I know you love me so much because

DEAR **SON,**

Tell me about a school subject that's difficult for you.

Why do you think it feels so challenging?

How can I help make it easier?

DRAW HOW
YOU FEEL
ABOUT IT.

DEAR **DAD,**

What do you think of what I wrote about school?

PERFECT TIME
FOR A HUG

Tell me about the subject you struggled with.

How does knowing that subject help you now?

YOU & ME

Five things that make us grin

SON

1 _____
2 _____
3 _____
4 _____
5 _____

DAD

1 _____
2 _____
3 _____
4 _____
5 _____

WE WRITE

DEAR **DAD,**

How did I get my name?

DEAR
SON,

I have a question for you

GOOD TIME
TO SAY HOW
YOU FEEL!

Date

DAD WRITES

Son, I always hear you say these expressions

SON WRITES

Dad, I always hear you say these expressions

DAD WRITES

I'm proud to be your dad because

_____

_____

_____

_____

I would describe you as a person who

_____

_____

_____

_____

You make me feel special when

_____

_____

_____

_____

SON WRITES

I'm proud to be your son because

_____

_____

_____

_____

I would describe you as a person who

_____

_____

_____

_____

You make me feel special when

_____

_____

_____

_____

DEAR DAD,

What are some of your favorite parts of being a dad?

NICE SPOT
TO DOODLE.

DEAR
SON,

What are your thoughts on
what I wrote about fatherhood?

Do you think you want to be a parent someday?

YOU & ME

The funniest person we know

DAD

SON

The bravest person we know

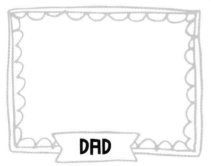

DAD

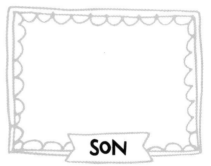

SON

The most generous person we know

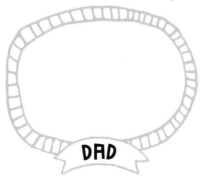

DAD

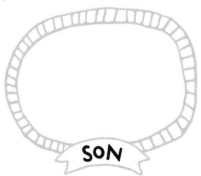

SON

DEAR **DAD,**

What was your first email address?

How did you get that name?

When did you get your first phone?
What did you use it for?

DRAW YOUR PHONE HERE.

Did your parents ever take away
your technology privileges? Why?

_____

_____

_____

_____

What did you do without today's technology?

_____

_____

_____

DEAR SON,

Record your current email
or username here.

How did you get that name?

Which platforms do you use it for?

How do you use those platforms and how often?

DRAW YOUR DEVICE HERE.

Do you ever feel pressured or
uncomfortable about anything online?

_____

_____

_____

_____

Is there anything I can do to help you when that happens?

_____

_____

DEAR **DAD,**

What are your thoughts on what I wrote
about feeling pressure or discomfort?

SON WRITES

Dad, in 30 years, you'll be _____ years old. If you remember just one thing about who I am today, I hope it's

_____

_____

_____

_____

_____

_____

DAD WRITES

Son, in 30 years, you'll be _____ years old. If you remember just one thing about who I am today, I hope it's

_____

_____

_____

_____

_____

_____

Here's a picture of
YOU & ME
doing something we love.

WE WRITE

YOU & ME

A person we admire

DAD

SON

A person we trust

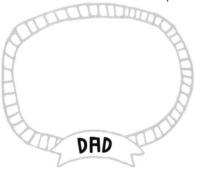

DAD

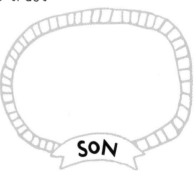

SON

A person we love

DAD

SON

DEAR **DAD,**

I have a question for you

_____

_____

_____

PERFECT TIME
FOR A HUG.

i ♥ u

SON WRITES

My typical weekday

6:00

7:00

8:00

9:00

10:00

11:00

NOON

1:00

2:00

3:00

4:00

5:00

6:00

7:00

8:00

9:00

10:00

DAD WRITES

My typical weekday

6:00

7:00

8:00

9:00

10:00

11:00

NOON

1:00

2:00

3:00

4:00

5:00

6:00

7:00

8:00

9:00

10:00

Here's a picture of
YOU & ME
soaking up summer.

We give summer ☆ ☆ ☆ ☆ ☆ stars!

FILL IN FOR RATING.

WE WRITE

- ☐ We love this season!
- ☐ Summer's just not long enough.
- ☐ LET THE SUN SHINE.
- ☐ The air conditioner is running.
- ☐ We should vacation somewhere _____er.
- ☐ Give us all the icy _____ to drink.
- ☐ We own _____ bottles of sunblock.
- ☐ _____

Our summer theme song should be

The best things to do each summer are

1 _____

2 _____

3 _____

4 _____

5 _____

DEAR SON,

Do you have any questions about growing up?

What are you excited about?

Is there anything you're nervous about?

How do you feel about your body right now?

When do you feel confident about your body?

Do you ever get uncomfortable about your appearance?

DEAR **DAD,**

What do you think about what I just wrote?

_____

_____

_____

_____

_____

_____

_____

Have you ever felt uncomfortable about your body?

_____

_____

_____

When do you feel confident about your body?

_____

_____

_____

Do you have any suggestions to help me become more comfortable or confident?

_____

_____

_____

_____

_____

_____

_____

What do you appreciate about being a grown man?

_____

_____

_____

_____

_____

_____

DEAR SON,

Tell me about a sport you enjoy.

What do you like about it?

How do you feel when you're doing it?

DEAR DAD,

What are your thoughts on what
I just wrote about my favorite sport?

Tell me about a sport you really enjoyed
when you were my age.

SON WRITES

Dad, I'll always ask for your advice on

_____

_____

_____

_____

I've always appreciated how you

_____

_____

_____

_____

I hope that you never stop

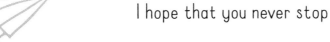

_____

_____

_____

_____

DAD WRITES

Son, I'll always ask for your advice on

I've always appreciated how you

I hope that you never stop

YOU  ME

If we had the whole day to spend together

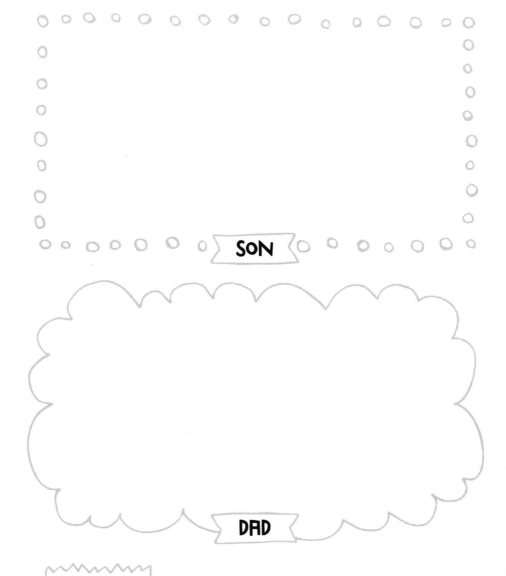

SON

DAD

WE WRITE

YOU ♥ ME

We know how to fix a

DAD

SON

People can count on us to

DAD

SON

We're totally capable of

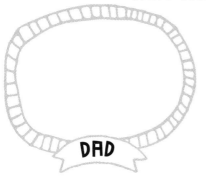

DAD

SON

SON WRITES

My favorite **HOLIDAY** is

because _____

_____

_____

_____

_____

_____

Here's us **CELEBRATING!**

DAD WRITES

My favorite **HOLIDAY** is

because _____

_____

_____

_____

_____

Here's us **CELEBRATING!**

DEAR **SON,**

Tell me about a hobby you enjoy.

How did you get interested in it?

What do you like about it?

What's challenging right now?

How would you rank this hobby?
I give this hobby ☆☆☆☆☆ stars!

 FILL IN FOR RATING.

DEAR **DAD,**

Tell me about a hobby you enjoy.

How did you get interested in it?

What do you like about it?

What's challenging right now?

How would you rank this hobby?
I give this hobby ☆☆☆☆☆ stars!

FILL IN FOR RATING.

SON  WRITES

Dad, this is you when

SOMEONE MAKES YOU LAUGH

YOU'RE IN YOUR ROOM

YOU DISCOVER I'VE WRITTEN
IN OUR JOURNAL

YOU GET A PACKAGE FROM

DAD WRITES

Son, this is you when

SOMEONE MAKES YOU LAUGH

YOU'RE IN YOUR ROOM

YOU DISCOVER I'VE WRITTEN IN OUR JOURNAL

YOU GET A PACKAGE FROM

DAD WRITES

Here's a keepsake from my life right now

It's a

- ☐ ticket stub
- ☐ receipt
- ☐ wrapper
- ☐ newspaper clipping

- ☐ quote or poem
- ☐ list or note from my pocket
- ☐ photo or picture
- ☐ _____

I'm adding it to our journal because

SON WRITES

Here's a keepsake from my life right now

It's a

- ☐ ticket stub
- ☐ receipt
- ☐ wrapper
- ☐ thing from school
- ☐ quote or poem
- ☐ list or note from my pocket
- ☐ photo or picture
- ☐ _____

I'm adding it to our journal because

DEAR
SON,

Do you remember a story
from when you were little?

ADD YOUR
STORY
DOODLES HERE.

SON WRITES

The money we have has enabled our family to

_____

_____

_____

These are times when money
doesn't matter to our family

_____

_____

_____

I think it's important to set aside money for

_____

_____

_____

I enjoy giving time or money to

_____

_____

_____

DAD WRITES

The money we have has enabled our family to

_____

_____

_____

These are times when money
doesn't matter to our family

_____

_____

_____

I think it's important to set aside money for

_____

_____

_____

I enjoy giving time or money to

_____

_____

_____

_____

DEAR **DAD,**

What was your most interesting job before I was born?

How old were you? And how much did you get paid?

How did you travel to and from work?

What were your responsibilities?

What made the job interesting and why did you stop?

Tell me about a mistake you made or lesson you learned.

DEAR **SON,**

What do you think about my favorite job?

Would you try it?

What kind of jobs do you want to experience?

Tell me about the kind of life you dream
of having when you're grown up.

DEAR **DAD,**

Tell me about an older relative that
I didn't get to know well.

DAD WRITES

ADD MEMORIES
AROUND THE
PICTURE FRAME.

SON WRITES

Dad, two things you did that made
me laugh or smile this past week

1

2

Two things other people did that
made me happy this past week

1

2

Two things I did this past week that hopefully
brought other people happiness

1

2

 **DAD** WRITES

Son, two things you did that made
me laugh or smile this past week

1 _____

2 _____

Two things other people did that
made me happy this past week

1 _____

2 _____

Two things I did this past week that hopefully
brought other people happiness

1 _____

2 _____

DEAR **DAD,**

Tell me about the first time you held me.

YOU ❤ ME

An activity we want to do together

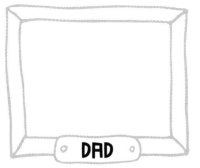

DAD

SON

An event we want to attend together

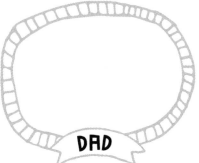

DAD

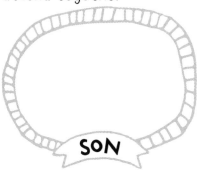

SON

A local place we want to go to together

DAD

SON

DAD WRITES

Son, when you're _____ years old like I am now,

make sure you take time for yourself to

_____

_____

_____

_____

_____

SON WRITES

Dad, when I'm _____ years old like you are now,

make sure you take time for yourself to

_____

_____

_____

_____

_____

DEAR DAD,

Do you vote? Why or why not?

What makes a good candidate, in your opinion?

SON WRITES
FUTURE PREDICTIONS

YOU AND ME IN _____ YEARS

Dad, I anticipate you won't have to spend
any more time on

_____

_____

_____

You'll have more time to

_____

_____

You'll be really good at

I'll have to start reminding you to

Most likely, you'll still be reminding me to

We'll still be laughing about that time when

DAD WRITES
FUTURE PREDICTIONS

YOU AND ME IN _____ YEARS

Son, I anticipate you won't have to spend
any more time on

_____

_____

_____

You'll have more time to

_____

_____

You'll be really good at

I'll have to start reminding you to

Most likely, you'll still be reminding me to

We'll still be laughing about that time when

★ ★ SON WRITES ★ ★

If I knew I could never fail, I would

★ ★ DAD WRITES ★ ★

Son, here's what I know about following your dreams

YOU & ME

A typical dinner scene at our house

DAD

SON

I could spend the whole weekend doing nothing but

I'm lucky because

The worst chore I have to do is

When I was a kid, I loved to spend my time

I could spend the whole weekend doing nothing but

_____

_____

_____

I'm lucky because

_____

_____

_____

The worst chore I have to do is

_____

_____

_____

When I'm an adult, I will spend my weekends

_____

_____

_____

DEAR _____,

I have a question for you

_____

_____

_____

WE WRITE

Son, let me trace your hand here.

SON WRITES

Dad, let me trace your hand here.

YOU  ME

We feel ready for summer when we wear

DAD

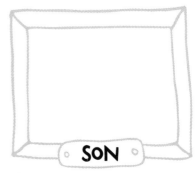
SON

We feel empowered when we wear

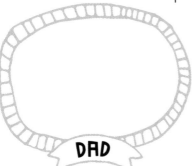
DAD

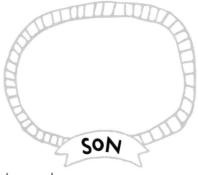
SON

We feel most like ourselves when we wear

DAD

SON

DEAR
SON,

Tell me what else is on your mind.

Here's a picture of
YOU ♥ ME
being _____.

DEAR SON,

YAHOO! We've reached the end of this journal. What did you enjoy about writing together?

How should we celebrate our journal's completion?

What will we do with our journal?

What do you want to do together next?

LET'S CELEBRATE YOUR STORY!

I believe that your story is one of the most
meaningful gifts you can give yourself and
the people you love. Thank you for entrusting
me and this journal with your adventures.
If you loved writing in these pages, let's celebrate
more of your story with my other books.
They're just as empowering and, well, awesome!

♡ Katie

LOVE, **MOM** AND **ME:** A Mother & Daughter Keepsake Journal

BETWEEN **MOM** AND **ME:** A Mother & Son Keepsake Journal

LOVE, **DAD** AND **ME:** A Father & Daughter Keepsake Journal

AWAITING **YOU:** A Pregnancy Journal

DISCOVER EVEN MORE KATIE CLEMONS
JOURNALS AT KATIECLEMONS.COM!